Project Management Drabble

10 Challenges of PM'ing
… and a Little Advice

Written by
Dawne E. Chandler, PhD

DEDICATION

To my family who inspires me to continually learn, grow, and share the experiences!

ACKNOWLEDGMENTS

Thank you to the executives, managers, project managers, and project teams that I have worked with over the years for the countless memorable moments to draw upon. Special thanks to the following Project Management Professionals (PMPs) for their reviews and valuable feedback: Mary Capra, Lisa Cooney, and Bill Knowles.

CONTENTS

Dedication & Acknowledgement i

Preface 1

1 Attaining the Right Sponsor 2

2 Securing Clear Direction 4

3 Discovering Stakeholders 6

4 Unearthing the Right Team 8

5 Assembling a Cohesive Plan 10

6 Conveying Consistent Messages 12

7 Detecting Risks 14

8 Negotiating Changes 16

9 Resolving Conflict 18

10 Closing the Project 20

PREFACE

What's a Project Management Drabble?

A whimsical way to highlight and share in 100 words, through ten cartoons and their 10-word captions, my experiences with the challenges senior managers and project managers encounter when striving to make their projects successful.

Who might enjoy this book?

Senior Management
Project Sponsors
Project Managers
Project Team Members
Stakeholders

How might this drabble be used?

You might use this drabble and its relatable cartoons to help get a sensitive message across when one of the ten challenges arises. The book can be an especially helpful "Go-To" for project managers looking for fun ways to express their frustrations and find advice on how to tackle a challenge. It can also be a handy reference for senior managers who perform project sponsorship and mentoring responsibilities to remind them, in a humorous way, what their project managers are up against and how they might help. For project team members and stakeholders, this book can expose them to ten common project challenges and encourage them to help prevent these project team issues before they arise!

Advice

- Ensure your organization has clearly defined roles and responsibilities for project sponsors and training on expected behavior. If not, then create them!

- If assigned a sponsor, then schedule time to go over both of your roles and responsibilities. Don't be afraid to explain what you need and expect of this role and be prepared to negotiate.

- If you can choose a sponsor, then assess what is needed and seek out an individual that can provide that type of support.

Who is the best person to fulfill this sponsorship role?

Advice

- Ask "This project will be complete when the team delivers what by when?" Answers to these questions help define metrics for success.

- Be proactive and don't be afraid to ask your project sponsor for clarification of objectives. Make sure you and your sponsor are clear on the timings and deadlines.

- Keep asking the sponsor for clarity until you are comfortable you understand the expectations for all the deliverables before starting to build the project plan.

**We really need clearer direction about
what they want done!**

Advice

- Evaluate your stakeholders and determine how each will help or hinder your project.
- Categorize each stakeholder and develop a plan that manages their expectations. Know their "Hot Buttons!"
- Communicate with all stakeholders! Don't shy away from the ones who are not supportive. It is key to know what your stakeholders are thinking and address their concerns along the way.
- Leverage stakeholder discussion opportunities to kick your relationship building skills into high gear!

Who will get in the way and who will
help?

Advice

- Talk to each team member to ensure this assignment is a good fit for them skill-wise and time-wise.
- Determine their attitude toward being on the team … Are they upset being assigned to the project, bored with it, delighted to be on the team, or avoid taking on new responsibilities whenever they can?
- Replace assigned team members that don't meet your objectives.
- Negotiate for resources when you are unable to get the skills you need when you need them.
- Develop a resource risk response plan.

It doesn't look like they all want to be
team-members?

Advice

- Solicit input early and often from your stakeholders and team members.

- Ensure you have a "big picture" view of the solution – as an example, using a mind map is a great tool for developing the "big picture" view.

- Test your plan by asking "If we do these things in this timeframe, will we arrive at the desired deliverables?"

There seems to be some missing pieces to
the plan?

Advice

- Utilize a communication vehicle that serves the masses; avoid using multiple delivery tools to deliver the same message as efficiency and effectiveness is your goal.

- If a project communication process doesn't exist then develop one that meets your needs and those of your stakeholders and team members.

- Be prepared to negotiate who gets what information and how often, so you don't end up with multiple ways to communicate the same message!

We need a consistent way to communicate
the project status!

Advice

- You don't want surprises, so risk planning is essential!
- If one doesn't exist, create a project culture where identifying risks is expected and the right thing to do. It's everyone's job to identify risk, not just the project manager.
- Garner sponsor support to get the message across to the project team that we need to know about all risks so we can proactively and collectively put the best risk response plans in place.
- If one doesn't exist, create a risk management plan process that incorporates stakeholders, sponsor, and project team member participation – from identification to risk plan creation through review, approvals, and escalation.

**Please help us identify ALL the risks to
the project!**

Advice

- As the Project Manager, provide options as a result of a pending change request! It's your job to consult!

- Be consultative as the decision lies with the customer (internal or external).

- Approach your negotiation by saying, "If we do Option A this is what will happen to schedule, cost, quality etc. Or, if we do Option B, this will happen. Or, Option C, etc." Then ask the customer, "What would you like to do?"

If you want plan changes, let's discuss the impact options?

Advice

- As the mediator, you need to understand all sides of the issue in order to negotiate a resolution that can satisfy all parties.
- Don't let conflict amongst team members fester – know when to intervene and when to let team members work it out.
- Create a project environment where expressing differing opinions is healthy.

Do I intervene or can they resolve the issue themselves?

Advice

- Set expectations at the kickoff meeting for project close-out requirements, such as documenting lessons learned or assigning open items.

- Engage sponsor support at the kickoff meeting to establish the importance of project closure tasks!

- Create project close-out items as tasks in your project schedule so team members see what needs to be accomplished.

- Have a formal project close-out meeting and ensure the sponsor attends. Celebrate success, making the close-out meeting fun with recaps and recognition to demonstrate the value received from the team members' time spent completing the close-out items!

We need to get this stuff done before moving on!

Project Management

"Drabble"

(Cartoon Captions = Exactly 100 words
to convey top challenges of managing projects)

- Who is the best person to fulfill this sponsorship role?

- We really need clearer direction about what they want done!

- Who will get in the way and who will help?

- It doesn't look like they all want to be team-members?

- There seems to be some missing pieces to the plan?

- We need a consistent way to communicate the project status!

- Please help us identify ALL the risks to the project!

- If you want plan changes, let's discuss the impact options?

- Do I intervene or can they resolve the issue themselves?

- We need to get this stuff done before moving on!

ABOUT THE AUTHOR

"Dr. Dawne" lives in Northern California with her husband.
She holds a PhD in Organization and Management with a specialization in
Project Management from Capella University and a MBA and BS from
Syracuse University. With 35-plus years of corporate experience, Dawne
retired recently to build her consulting practice, publish, and teach. Her last
position was the Vice President of Operations at DST Output, one of the
nation's largest print/mail and electronic outsourcing firms, overseeing
strategic planning and their national project management office (PMO).
There she held various executive positions in sales/marketing, product and
process re-engineering, and heading an electronic services start-up. Before,
she spent 18 years at IBM in various technical, sales, consulting, and
management positions. She is a Certified Project Management Professional
(PMP). Dawne presented at the PMI Research and Education Conference
2014 on the topic "Does Executive Sponsorship Matter for Realizing
Project Management Value?"

www.ingramcontent.com/pod-product-compliance
Lightning Source LLC
Chambersburg PA
CBHW070757180526
45168CB00004B/1646